The Happy House

Written by Jill Eggleton
Illustrated by Philip Webb

The people on Harriet's street did not smile.
They did not look happy.

The cats did not purr.
The dogs did not bark
and the birds did not sing.

"I will make a happy house," said Harriet.
So Harriet painted her house purple and green.

She painted a big
yellow sun on the roof
and a big yellow smile
on the door.

Harriet put tables and chairs in her garden.
She put up blue umbrellas.

She painted big yellow suns
on the umbrellas
and a big yellow smile
on her mailbox.

Harriet put on purple shoes and a green skirt. She painted a big yellow sun on her hat and a big yellow smile on her shirt.

She made a sign and put it on her gate...

The people on the street came to Harriet's house. Harriet gave them coffee in blue cups with yellow smiles, and they laughed.

The dogs on the street
came to Harriet's house.
Harriet gave them cakes
and they wagged their tails.

The cats on the street came to Harriet's house. Harriet gave them cakes and they purred.

The birds came
to Harriet's house.
They sat on
the blue umbrellas.
Harriet gave them cakes
and they sang.

"Good!" said Harriet.
"There are happy people.
There are happy dogs and
happy cats and happy birds.
This **is** a happy house."

Thank-you Notes

Guide Notes

Title: The Happy House
Stage: Early (2) – Yellow

Genre: Fiction
Approach: Guided Reading
Processes: Thinking Critically, Exploring Language, Processing Information
Written and Visual Focus: Thank-you notes

THINKING CRITICALLY
(sample questions)
- What do you think this story could be about?
- Focus on the title. What do you think could be meant by a "Happy House?"
- Why do you think the people in the house were not happy?
- Look at the colors Harriet is using. Why do you think she is choosing yellow, purple, and green?
- What do you think made the people, the animals, and the birds happy?

EXPLORING LANGUAGE

Terminology
Title, cover, illustrations, author, illustrator

Vocabulary
Interest words: happy, umbrella, purred
High-frequency words (reinforced): the, in, did, not, look, and, I, will, make, house, said, so, her, on, big, put, for, with, they, there, this, is, a
New words: made, people, gave, came, them

Print Conventions
Capital letter for sentence beginnings and names (**H**arriet), periods, quotation marks, commas, ellipses